HISTORY RELIVED

The Tudors

W0011019

...oper

Photographs by Martyn F. Chillmaid

WAYLAND

HISTORY RELIVED

This book is a differentiated text version of *The Tudors* by Liz Gogerly.

Conceived and produced for Wayland by

Nutshell
MEDIA
www.nutshellmedialtd.co.uk

This edition first published in 2009 by Wayland.

© Copyright 2009 Nutshell Media Ltd

This paperback edition published in 2012 by Wayland

Editor: Polly Goodman
Original designer: Simon Borrough
Layout for this edition: Jane Hawkins
All reconstructions set up and photographed by: Martyn F. Chillmaid

British Library Cataloguing in Publication Data
Cooper, Alison, 1967-
The Tudors. -- Differentiated ed. -- (History relived)
1. Great Britain--History--Tudors, 1485-1603--Juvenile literature.
2. Great Britain--Social life and customs--16th century--Juvenile literature.
I. Title II. Series III. Gogerly, Liz. Tudors reconstructed.
942'.05-dc22

ISBN: 978 0 7502 6802 8

Printed and bound in China

Wayland is a division of Hachette Children's Books,
A Hachette UK Company

www.hachette.co.uk

Cover photographs: Top left: a boy shows off his wooden toy; Centre left: musicians play in a nobleman's house; Bottom left: a customer looks at some cheese at a market stall.
Right: a falconer stands with his bird.

Title page: A nobleman and his family enjoy a banquet.

The photographer wishes to thank the following for their help and assistance:
St Mawes Castle, Cornwall; Godolghan Garrison, Cornwall.

Contents

K+-362-240

Who Were the Tudors?

The first Tudor king was Henry VII. He became king in 1485. His children and grandchildren ruled England for more than 100 years.

When Henry VII died in 1509, his son Henry became King Henry VIII. Henry VIII enjoyed sport, music, dancing and feasting. He was young and popular when he first became king.

Later in his reign Henry made big changes to religion in England. He closed down monasteries, and gave the monastery land and treasures to men who supported him.

Some of Henry's supporters already had land and riches. Others became landowners and noblemen for the first time. The noblemen enjoyed their new wealth.

▶ A wealthy nobleman relaxes at home with his family.

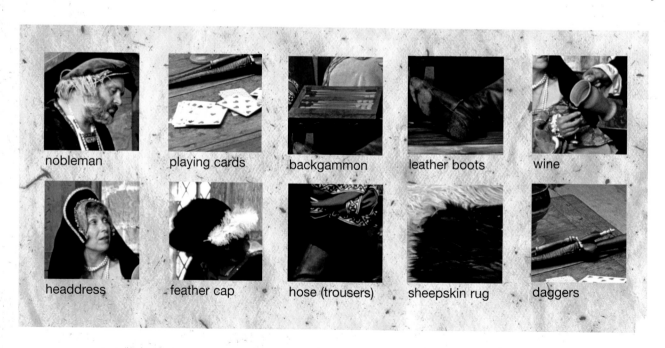

nobleman playing cards backgammon leather boots wine

headdress feather cap hose (trousers) sheepskin rug daggers

Riches for the Rich

Rich Tudors loved to show off their fine clothes and big houses.

Noblemen and noblewomen wore clothes made from velvets, silks and shiny taffeta. At one time it was fashionable to have cuts, called 'slashes', in the top layer of fabric. Colourful fabric beneath showed through the cuts. Very rich people added fur, gold thread and jewels to their clothes.

The nobles loved having long banquets. Some things they ate sound very strange today – badger, seagull, tortoise and otter. They would serve roast veal or venison to impress their guests. Dishes like these were washed down with expensive French wine.

jug of wine | silver cup

musician | wooden bowls

waiting staff | serving boy

▼ This noble family is enjoying a banquet.

6

Nobles had plenty of time for sports. They enjoyed hunting, jousting, tennis and bowls. In jousting, two men would gallop towards each other and try to knock each other off the horse with a lance.

Falconry was very popular, too. Birds of prey were trained to catch other birds and bring them back to their keeper. The wealthiest nobles kept the biggest and most expensive birds of prey. King Henry VIII had a gyr falcon.

▶ The falconer wears a leather glove to protect his arm from the buzzard's sharp talons.

leather glove   buzzard

dagger handle   slashed sleeves

Life for the Poor

Poor people did not have much time for games and sports. They had to work hard to earn a living.

In Tudor times, most people lived in the countryside and farmed the land. Farm work began at dawn and carried on until it got dark. Farm labourers worked six days a week. They only had a holiday when there was a church festival, such as a saint's day.

The main food that poor people ate was bread. They made soups and stews from vegetables and herbs. Some people kept a cow or goat so that they could have milk and cheese. They kept hens to give them eggs.

◀ Women fetched water in buckets from the nearest well. The buckets were very heavy when they were full.

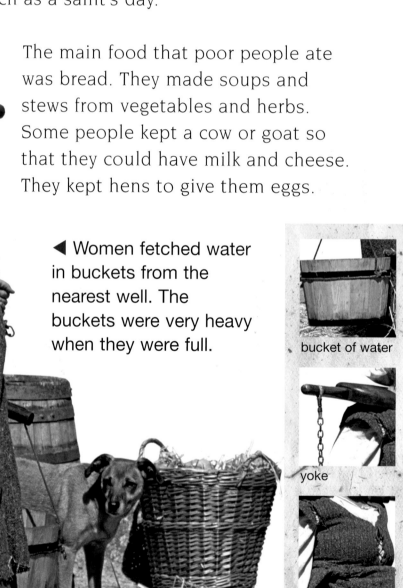

bucket of water

yoke

woollen dress

pillory	guard	market stall	dung	villager

▲ A boy throws dung at a man in the pillory.

Villagers worked together and helped each other in difficult times. People who stole or did other crimes were punished. They might have to stand in the pillory – a wooden device that locked a criminal's hands and head between two boards. The villagers threw dung and rotten food at them. Travelling beggars, called vagabonds, might be beaten and then forced out of the village.

Dirt and Disease

The Tudors did not know how diseases spread and how dangerous dirt could be.

In the towns, houses were crammed close together. Most people threw their waste into open drains in the middle of the street. Animal dung, waste from the butcher's shop, dirty water, sewage – it all ended up in the streets.

◄ These women are washing clothes in a river. They rub the clothes with soap and beat them against rocks to get the dirt out. Then they rinse them and spread them on the bushes to dry.

Drinking water in streams and wells was often polluted. People became ill and many died. Sickness could spread quickly through the crowded houses.

Plague was one of the most terrifying diseases. It was spread by fleas that lived on rats. The only way people could protect themselves from it was to keep away from people who were sick.

▲ A servant pours dirty water out into the street.

dirty water

timber-framed house

latticed windows

beams for support

Wealth from Wool

Sheep were very important to the Tudors. They provided work for many craftspeople and made some Tudors very wealthy.

Shepherds had the job of caring for the sheep. They carried a crook to catch the sheep and shears to cut their fleeces.

Once the fleeces had been cut and cleaned, spinners got to work. They spun the wool into thread and weavers wove the thread into cloth. Dyers coloured the cloth and tailors made it into clothing. A lot of wool and cloth was sold to other countries.

▲ A shepherd watches over some sheep.

crook

woollen cap

woollen tunic

woollen leggings

Landowners who owned the sheep became very rich. So did the merchants who sold the wool. They could afford grand houses built of stone, instead of wooden houses.

The new houses were built by stonemasons. These were craftsmen who cut and shaped big blocks of stone so they could be used in new buildings. Each stonemason carved his own special symbol into the stone he worked on. This was to make sure he got paid for all his work.

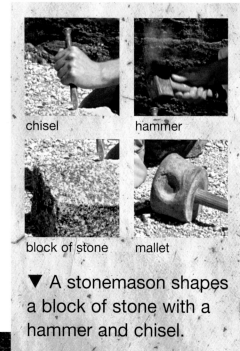

chisel   hammer

block of stone   mallet

▼ A stonemason shapes a block of stone with a hammer and chisel.

Women's Work

Housework was hard work in Tudor times. Running the home kept women very busy.

Women got up early to begin their chores. They cooked, washed and cleaned. They made soap and candles. In the countryside, women churned milk to make butter and cheese, and collected honey.

pig on spit   basket of apples   wooden barrels

lantern   sack of wool   spindle

▼ These cooks are preparing a feast in the kitchen of the manor house.

▲ A customer checks some cheese at a market stall.

Food shopping was usually done at the local market. There, women could buy meat, eggs, cheese and vegetables.

Women had paid jobs, too. In the towns, they worked as cooks, servants, weavers, shopkeepers and barmaids. Some women travelled from village to village, selling lace and other goods.

In Tudor times, people believed that women were weaker and less important than men. Women were expected to do what their husbands told them to do.

customer

stallholder

apples

cheese

bread

eggs and vegetables

Tudor Children

In Tudor times, girls were mainly educated at home. Boys went to school if their families could afford to pay for it. Poor children did not go to school at all.

Boys started school when they were four. There were not many books. Pupils read from hornbooks. These were wooden boards with writing pinned to them. They were covered with a transparent layer of cow's horn.

Some girls from wealthy families had tutors and were very well educated. But most girls learned how to run a home rather than how to read Latin and Greek.

hornbook

Latin book

woollen doublet

woollen breeches

▼ A teacher listens as his pupil reads aloud from a hornbook.

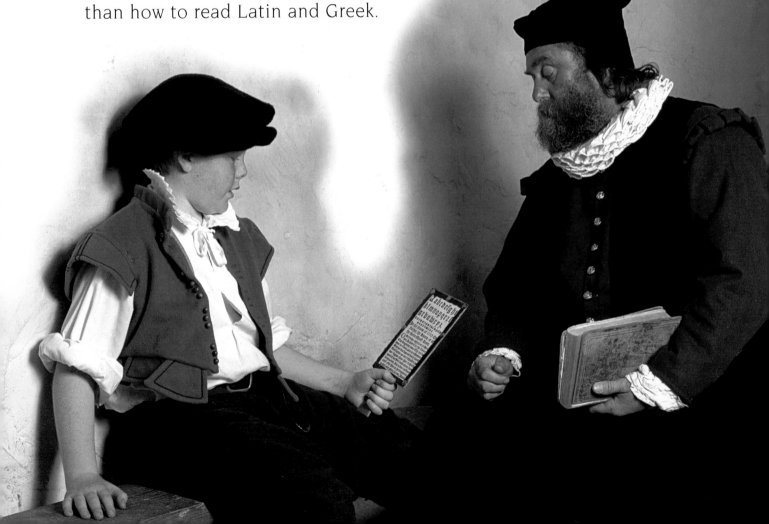

▲ A boy shows off a new toy. It is a windmill that uses string to make the sails turn.

Children from poorer families started work by the age of six or seven. Many helped their families. Some boys became apprentices to craftsmen. They spent seven years learning the skills of their master.

Tudor children still had time to play. Sometimes their parents carved wooden toys for them. Children made their own toys, too. They blew up pigs' bladders for footballs and made hoops from old barrels. They enjoyed games such as blind man's buff and leapfrog.

▼ Some popular Tudor toys.

spinning tops

bear on a stick

jack stones

windmill

clay marbles

dolls

Fighting for England

There had been years of war in England before Henry VII became king. The Tudors brought peace to England, but they had many enemies abroad.

King Henry VIII was worried that France would try to invade England. He had new castles built along the south coast. He ordered new ships for the navy, too. In 1545, some French soldiers landed in England, but Henry's troops defeated them.

▼ Soldiers practise with their weapons high up on the castle walls.

matchlock (gun)   match

armour   sword handle

longbow and arrow   bill

In 1588, when Elizabeth I was Queen, England faced an attack from Spain. The King of Spain tried to send his army to England in a great fleet of ships called the Armada.

The English set fire to some of their own ships and sailed them into the Spanish fleet. Some Spanish ships were burned. A few were sunk in battle. Many more were sunk by a great storm. England was safe.

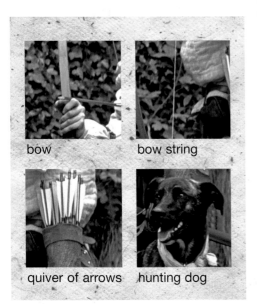

bow   bow string

quiver of arrows   hunting dog

▲ English archers were famous for their skill with longbows like these. Longbows could be used for hunting as well as fighting.

Religious Trouble

England had been a Catholic country for hundreds of years. The head of the Catholic Church was the Pope. Everyone, even kings and queens, obeyed the Pope.

In 1533, King Henry VIII decided that he wanted to divorce his wife, Katherine. The Catholic Church and the Pope would not let him. So in 1534, Henry announced that he was going to be head of the Church in England and he split from the Catholic Church.

Catholic priest   Latin Bible

family members   altar

▼ A Catholic family attends a service in secret in their home.

priest

soldier

dagger

◀ A soldier discovers a Catholic priest hiding in someone's home.

After 1534, people in England were made to worship in a new way. They could not use Bibles written in Latin any more – only Bibles written in English. Statues and paintings of saints were taken out of churches.

Life became very dangerous for people who did not want to worship in the new way. During Queen Elizabeth I's reign, it was against the law for Catholic priests to live in England. Many went to live abroad, but some carried on holding services in secret. Priests who were caught were tortured and sometimes killed.

Explorers

In the reign of Queen Elizabeth I, explorers made long voyages across the oceans.

One of the most famous explorers was Sir Francis Drake. In 1577 he set out in his ship, the *Golden Hind*, and sailed right around the world. His journey took three years.

Drake returned to England with a rich cargo of gold. He had stolen this from Spanish ships and settlements in South America. The Spanish complained that Drake was a pirate. But Queen Elizabeth did not mind because Drake gave lots of the gold to her!

Sir Humphrey Gilbert was another explorer. He planned to set up the first English settlement in North America. In 1583 he landed in Newfoundland, which is part of Canada today. But he did not stay there long enough to make a settlement. On the voyage home his ship sank and he drowned.

▶ A group of explorers take a look around. They have just landed on the coast of Newfoundland.

officer in charge   pistol   bill   pikeman

standard   archer   sword   halberd

Entertainment

▲ Musicians play in a nobleman's house.

Music, dancing and plays were important to the rich and the poor in Tudor times.

Musicians and actors travelled around the country. Some gave performances in the homes of wealthy nobles. They played instruments that were easy to carry around. The *viola da braccio* was like a modern violin. The lute and the cittern were like guitars.

King Henry VIII loved music. Some experts think he wrote the love song 'Greensleeves', which people still sing today.

viola da braccio

lute

cittern

hurdy-gurdy

harp

bagpipe

Queen Elizabeth I enjoyed dancing. She loved to flirt with the young men at her court.

Poor people did not have much free time, but they made the most of their holidays. In the spring, Morris men would arrive in the villages. Their dances celebrated the arrival of spring and new life.

In early Tudor times, actors performed their plays in the yards of inns. The first theatre opened in London in 1576. It was called 'The Theatre'. More theatres opened soon after. William Shakespeare wrote some of the plays that were performed there.

bells   ribbons

woollen shirt   woollen waistcoat

hurdy-gurdy   villager

▼ Morris dancers perform in the village square.

In the Tavern

In some ways, going to the tavern was like going to the pub today.

Most taverns had a painted sign outside, such as a golden lion, a black horse or a white swan. The signs were useful for people who could not read. They could arrange to meet 'under the sign of the red lion', for instance. At the tavern, people could get a drink and a hot meal. They could enjoy a game of cards or dice.

Alehouses were rougher places than taverns. People might gather there to watch a cock fight. They would bet money on which cockerel would win. There were other fights, too, between dogs and bears, or dogs and badgers. The Tudors enjoyed these shows, which seem very cruel to us today.

The crowded, noisy taverns and alehouses could be dangerous places. Drunken fights were common. One famous playwright, Christopher Marlowe, was stabbed to death in a fight in a tavern.

▶ Customers in a tavern enjoy some pigs' trotters and a game of draughts.

draughts   fighting cockerel   barrel of wine   pig's trotters   wooden tankard

pot of salt   bread   purse   shopping sack   pewter tankard

Timeline

1485

Henry Tudor kills King Richard III at the Battle of Bosworth. He becomes King Henry VII, the first Tudor ruler.

1509

Henry VII dies. His son becomes King Henry VIII.

1516

Henry's wife, Queen Katherine, gives birth to Mary.

1533

Henry divorces Katherine and marries Anne Boleyn. Anne gives birth to Elizabeth.

1534

Henry makes himself head of the Church of England.

1536

Henry begins closing down the monasteries. He has Anne Boleyn beheaded. He marries Jane Seymour.

1537

Jane Seymour gives birth to Edward. She dies soon after.

1540

Henry marries Anne of Cleves. He soon decides that he does not like her and quickly divorces her. Then he marries Katherine Howard.

1542

Katherine Howard is executed. Henry marries Katherine Parr.

1545

A French army tries to invade England. The attack fails.

1547

Henry VIII dies. His son becomes King Edward VI. He is only nine years old.

1553

Edward dies at the age of 16. His half-sister becomes Queen Mary I.

1558

Mary dies. Her half-sister becomes Elizabeth I.

1576

James Burbage opens the first theatre in London, called 'The Theatre'.

1577

Francis Drake sets out on his round-the-world voyage.

1588

The English navy defeats the Spanish Armada.

1603

Queen Elizabeth I dies. She is the last Tudor monarch.

Glossary

apprentice A person who is learning a job. Tudor apprentices usually spent seven years being taught by an expert.

archers People who fight with bows and arrows.

banquet A large meal with lots of different dishes. Tudor banquets could last for hours.

beam A thick piece of wood that helps to hold up a building.

bill A pole with a sharp blade at the end, curved into a hook.

bladder Part of the body that holds waste liquid (urine).

blind man's buff A game in which one person is blindfolded and then has to try to catch the other players.

breeches Short trousers that reach to a person's knees.

Catholic A Christian who accepts the Pope as head of the Church. It is also a word to describe a particular way of worshipping God.

cock fight A fight between two cockerels.

crook A long, thick stick with a curved hook at one end.

doublet A tight-fitting jacket.

dung Toilet waste from animals.

halberd A pole with an axe blade on one side and a hook on the other. The hook was used to pull mounted soldiers off their horses.

hurdy-gurdy An instrument that was played by turning a handle and pressing keys at the same time.

latticed window A window with a criss-cross pattern made from strips of lead. It was very common in Tudor buildings.

longbow A very tall bow that could fire arrows over long distances.

monastery A place where monks lived. Monks were men who had promised to spend their lives praying, thinking about God and, sometimes, helping the poor and sick.

noblemen Rich, powerful men who owned large areas of land.

pewter A mixture of metals that is a dull grey colour.

pike A very long wooden pole (more than 3 metres long) with a sharp metal point on the end.

playwright A person who writes plays.

reign The period of time that begins when a person becomes king or queen and lasts until they die.

sewage Toilet waste.

settlement A place where people live together, such as a village or a town.

standard A flag that has the personal symbols of a noble on it.

tankard A drinking cup.

timber-framed house A house that is built from thick beams of wood. This is the timber frame. The space between the beams is filled with thin, woven strips of wood and covered with clay and straw.

yoke A wooden bar that a person puts across their shoulders, with a load hanging from each end. It makes it easier to carry heavy loads.

Activities

pp4–5 Who Were the Tudors?

- Can you find out the names of all five Tudor kings and queens? Try to find a picture of each of them. Make a family tree poster using the pictures.

- Look at the picture on page 5. Do you recognise any games that are still played today?

pp6–7 Riches for the Rich

- Look at pictures of noblemen and noblewomen in this book, other books and the Internet. Can you find examples of 'slashing', fur trims, gold thread and jewels on their clothes?

- Design and write a menu for a Tudor banquet that has ten courses. Include some of the dishes that are described on page 6.

pp8–9 Life for the Poor

- Look at the woman on page 8. What jobs do you think she did each day to prepare food for her family?

- Use books or the Internet to find out about the different kinds of rogue in Tudor England. Look for abraham men, clapperdudgeons, counterfeit cranks and priggers of prancers! Draw some pictures of them.

pp10–11 Dirt and Disease

- Plague killed thousands of people in England in Tudor times. Use books or the Internet to find out more about plague. How did it spread? What happened to people who became ill?

- Using the information on page 10, imagine you have travelled back in time and are walking through a Tudor town. Write a postcard back home describing what you see and smell.

pp12–13 Wealth from Wool

- These are some of the great houses that were built in Tudor times: Compton Wynyates in Warwickshire, Wollaton Hall in Nottingham, Hardwick Hall in Derbyshire, Shibden Hall in Yorkshire. Look for pictures of them in books or on the Internet.

- Imagine you are a stonemason in Tudor times. Design your own symbol to carve into your work so that people will know it is yours.

pp14–15 Women's Work

- Look at the picture on page 14. What do you think it was like to work in that kitchen? What smells were there? What sounds were there? Was it hot or cold?

- Try growing some herbs that the Tudors used, such as parsley, mint, sage and dill. Can you find out how the Tudors used them and have a go yourself?

pp16–17 Tudor Children

- Compare your life to the lives of Tudor children. Write a list of the similarities and differences.

- Write a list of instructions that explain how to play the game blind man's bluff. Look in books or on the Internet if you need more help.

pp18–19 Fighting for England

- There were no telephones or electricity in Queen Elizabeth's time. How do you think people found out that the Armada had nearly reached England? Use books or the Internet to help you.

- What ways can you think of to pass a message quickly?

pp20–21 Religious Trouble

- Find out about the wives of Henry VIII. Write down their names and the dates of each marriage in a chart.

- Imagine what it might have been like to be one of the Catholics in the picture on page 20. What might you think about having to worship in secret? How might you feel when the soldiers arrive to search the house?

pp22–23 Explorers

- These are some of the countries that Francis Drake visited on his voyage around the world: Argentina, Chile, Peru, California, Molucca Islands, Cape of Good Hope, Sierra Leone. Find these places on a world map or globe.

pp24–25 Entertainment

- Design a poster to advertise a new play at 'The Theatre', or to tell people when the Morris dancers will be coming to your village.

pp26–27 In the Tavern

- What do you think would be a good name for a tavern? Draw a sign for the tavern that people will easily understand and remember.

Find Out More

BOOKS TO READ

Building History: Tudor Theatre by Gillian Clements (Franklin Watts, 2008)

The Daily Life of a Tudor Criminal by Alan Childs (Wayland, 2008)

Historical Stories: Elizabeth I by Geoffrey Tease (Wayland, 2008)

Historical Stories: Henry VIII by Geoffrey Tease (Wayland, 2008)

Look Inside: A Shakespearean Theatre by Peter Chrisp (Wayland, 2007)

Look Inside: A Tudor Medicine Chest by Brian Moses (Wayland, 2007)

PLACES TO VISIT

Hampton Court, East Molesey, Surrey
www.hrp.org.uk/hamptoncourtpalace/
Visit the state apartments of Henry VIII, see a Tudor kitchen and explore the gardens and maze.

Mary Rose Museum Ship, Portsmouth
www.maryrose.org/
Visit this museum and see the only sixteenth-century warship on display in the world.

St Mawes Castle, Cornwall; Stokesay Castle, Shropshire; and Dartmouth Castle, Devon were all used for some of the photographs in this book.

Index

Page numbers in **bold** mean there is a photo on the page.